HAVE YOU SEEN MY SHEEP?

BOB HARTMAN

ILLUSTRATIONS BY

ROSIE MORGAN

CWR

For Gideon

Copyright © Bob Hartman 2015
Published 2015 by CWR, Waverley Abbey House, Waverley Lane,
Farnham, Surrey GU9 8EP, UK.
CWR is a Registered Charity – Number 294387 and a Limited
Company registered in England – Registration Number 1990308.
The right of Bob Hartman to be identified as the author of this
work has been asserted by him in accordance with the Copyright,
Designs and Patents Act 1988 sections 77 and 78.
All rights reserved. No part of this publication may be reproduced,
stored in a retrieval system, or transmitted, in any form or by
any means, electronic, mechanical, photocopying, recording or
otherwise, without the prior permission in writing of CWR.
Visit www.cwr.org.uk/distributors for a list of National Distributors.
Concept development, editing, design and production by CWR.
Illustrations by Rosie Morgan, visit rosiemorganart.com
Printed in the UK by Linney Group
ISBN: 978-1-78259-452-9

This Bible story is
found in Luke 15:4-7

Hello there.
That's right, you guessed it.
I'm a shepherd and these are my sheep.

Every now and then I count them, to make sure they're all safe. Here goes ...

... Ninety-seven, ninety-eight, ninety-nine.

Oh dear. There should be a hundred sheep.
You know what that means, don't you?

One of them is missing!

We need to find my lost sheep.

We'll start round here, in the hills.
Hopefully she hasn't gone far.

Right then. Into the woods we go. I know, it's a little scary in here. But we have to find my sheep.

I see it, too! And we'd better run.
That's definitely NOT my sheep!

Okay, we made it to the river. But what if my sheep fell in? Oh dear.

Over there? Yes.

But it's not my sheep. Phew!

I'm so pleased we found that little bridge.
Hopefully my sheep did, too.

Looks like we're in the vineyard, now.

Yes I see. Over there.
But it's still not my sheep.

Perhaps she wandered off to the farm. She does love to eat grass after all.

Oh yes, quite right,
but it's not my sheep.

Careful. We don't want to disturb anyone
in those houses. Can't imagine my sheep
is hiding here.

STILL, CAN YOU SEE ANYTHING THAT'S WHITE?

I see it, too.
But it's not my sheep.

The market is awfully crowded, today. There are people everywhere. And animals, too.

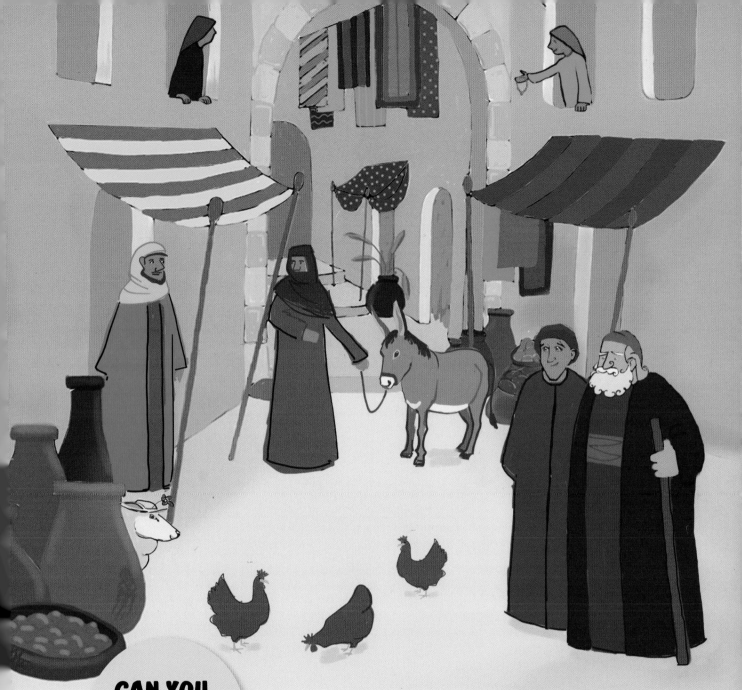

CAN YOU SEE ANY SHEEP?

Yes, I see it. But that one belongs to another shepherd. It's not *my* sheep.

Well, we've reached the boatyard. And there's nothing but the sea, beyond. So unless she's here, this is the end of the line.

Four legs.
A shaggy coat.
A sheepy shape.
Black nose.
Blue eyes.
Everything else white.
Grass in its mouth.

It's my sheep!

So off we go.

Back home to the
hills to put her
with the others.

It's party time!

All of my neighbours and friends are here. Singing and dancing and celebrating. I'm glad you could come too, after all, you helped so much!

LOST AND FOUND

Did you know that Jesus told this story about a lost sheep in the Bible? (You can find it in Luke 15:4–7.) And this story has something very important to teach us, because it's actually all about God and us. You see:

> **The shepherd = God.**
>
> **The sheep = you and me.**

Jesus wants us to understand that, without God in our lives, we are **lost**. But that's only the beginning of the story!

Just like the shepherd cared about his sheep, God cares deeply about you and me. He searches and searches for us in the hope that we may come to know Him and believe in Him.

Just like the shepherd found his sheep, we can be found.

Just like the shepherd threw a big party to celebrate, God throws a huge party in heaven every time someone comes to know Him as their Friend and Father.

If you want to know God as your Friend and Father, you can pray this prayer:

> **Dear God, I want to know You as my Father in heaven. I want to welcome You into my heart and follow Your way for the rest of my life. Amen.**

If you've prayed this prayer, and really meant it in your heart, then heaven is celebrating right now! For you were once lost but now you are **found**!

BONUS ROUND!

The next time you read this book, can you also find all of these items hidden in the pages?